COMMANDER IN CHIEF TROPHY

BY

PAUL H. D'ANNA

COPYRIGHTS

ISBN: 978-1-957837-84-0

ABOUT THE AUTHOR

Paul Henry D'Anna. AKA PHD

I was born on August 27,1943 in New Orleans Louisiana in the French Quarter.

I attended St. Louis Cathedral elementary school and De Las Salle High School. After graduating, I went to LSU and received a Bachelor's degree in Electrical Engineering. I was hired by IBM in Huntsville, Alabama, and programmed the IBM 360 computers. Next, I held positions at Shell Oil Company and Mobil Exxon. In 1992, I started my own business named "PC CONSULTANTS, I retired in 2010 from everyday work and started growing mirlitons, a vegetable native to Louisiana.

WHY DID I WRITE THIS BOOK?

In 1959, I read an article about cadets from West Point stealing the Navy's mascot. The NAVY goat. I thought that that was cool. I used to think of many ways to steal the goat and not get caught. I was inspired to write the book. In 1992, I read another article about Army cadets trying to steal the Navy goat again. At the same time, I read an unrelated article about the COMMANDER IN CHIEF's Trophy. I researched it, and I said to myself that it would be great if the trophy could be stolen.

As I followed Desert Storm, I was intrigued by the air war, especially "Operation Normandy"

.THEN CAME COVID 19.

With everything coming to a halt, I started adding more to my notes.

Finally, in 2021 I went crazy writing hour after hour, day after day.

All of a sudden, I had a book. I wondered if anyone else would enjoy reading it.

So, here it is.

FOREWORD

INTRODUCTION

PROLOGUE

TELL ABOUT THE BOOK

Table of Contents

Preface

DEDICATION

I dedicate this book to all of the men and women who have sacrificed themselves for the protection of our country and to my wife for her editing abilities and patients with my spelling.

I love and respect our military, and may GOD protect us and our military.

I also dedicate this book to my son Paul M D'Anna for his suggestions on the book cover.

ACKNOWLEDGEMENT

To my wonderful wife (Jane). Since she edited my first
grocery list, I knew she had an exceptional ability to correct
spelling errors, modify phrases, and bring out the intended
meaning of a paragraph. On many occasions, she would see
spelling errors and incorrect usage of sentences in TV
commercials.

THE NAVY GOAT BARN 1955

It is a cold and miserable night in 1955. Two army cadets are crawling towards their objective, a small building on a farm outside of Annapolis. It is surrounded by a small stockyard. "The snow is blowing sideways as they approach the barn; the leader of the group goes by the nickname of "Yag," and his sidekick, Frank T. Bluster, goes by the nickname "Phineas." (Phineas T. Bluster was a puppet character on the "HOWDY DOODY" TV show in the '50s.)

They crawl slowly to the barn. The door is closed but not locked. As it is opened, they see the object of their quest, the Navy goat. The goat gives a cry of distress as it is being taken out of the barn. The sound of the crying goat is muffled by the stormy winds. Slowly, they make their successful getaway, "Yag" pauses and smiles with great content. Phineas calls out. "Army First, Navy Last," "Army First, Navy Last," Army First, Navy Last," " Army First, Navy Last." They give each other a "Hi-five" as they drive away from the barn. The location where the goat was kept has never been revealed.

Back at the West Point campus, Cadet N. Schwarzkoph is studying different scenarios of battle engagements. He understands that there is not just one way to win a battle. If you are going to win, you need a plan that can change in an instant; Deception, Decoys, Speed, Retreat, Supplies, and Bluffs need to be incorporated into every plan. He makes a note about facing an enemy head-on, bluffing a direct attack while secretly preparing an attack around the flank. He labels his plan – "END RUN."

The dorm door opens, and there stands 'Yag.' "You are never going to believe what happened. Let me tell you what happened tonight." Schwarzkoph shakes his head.

The morning papers in Maryland treat the theft as perpetrated by a gang of thugs, while the NEW YORK newspapers treat them as heroes. "YAG" reads the papers and laughs.

Three days later, the goat is returned unharmed.

Peace reigns until 1989.

THE CALENDAR MOVES TO 1989

Six West Point cadets traveled to a farm near Annapolis, Maryland. It is the property of the U.S. Naval Academy. The Navy keeps its mascots there. The current mascot goes by the name of BILL 37.

Bill 37 belongs to a very long line of goats with the same name. All Bills before him and those who come after him will all stay at the same farm.

Kidnapping a mascot is a decades-long tradition amongst the service academies. And despite it being officially off-limits, a group of cadets decided to take **Bill No. 37** as their own.

It is mid-December 1989. The cadets are dressed in white and are carrying a large white blanket to cover the goat. The snow is blowing sideways. They are very tactful to avoid detection. As they approach their target, they split into two groups. The EXECUTION group - (Paul Toscano, John Little, and Sesay Swift) will attempt to take the Navy goat while the DECOY group - (Maximus Icon, P.M. Porto, and Chris Higginbottom) will distract the security guard.

Maximus Icon removes two packages from his knapsack. One is a small drone which he gives to Chris Higginbottom.

Chris starts the drone and guides it in front of the security guard. The guard reacts first surprised and then confused. As the guard approaches the drone, Chris hits the wrong switch, and the drone crashes into the door. Maximus Icon jumps into action. He has his own robot as a backup. It is a robot made to look like a talking goat with drums.

Tonight, the goat robot is dressed like an Admiral.

Maximus activates the robot and maneuvers it in front of the guard and hits its drums, and shouts, "THIS IS ADMIRAL RIDDICK. I NEED YOUR HELP WITH A PROBLEM AT THE MAIN HOUSE. FOLLOW ME." HUP TWO THREE FOUR, HUP TWO …………...

The cadet dutifully follows the robot goat in the direction of the large house.

Paul Toscano and John Little come out of their camouflage position and rush to the unprotected barn. With considerable effort, they pry open the lock on the barn door.

It's very dark, and the cadets are unaware that the Navy has many goats in the barn. Which one is Bill 37 (The Current Mascot)?

Without lights, John Little grabs the first goat he feels and covers it with the white blanket. John has kidnapped Bill 34, not Bill 37.

Bill 37, the current mascot, is youthful and of great health.

Bill 34, the goat that was kidnapped, is a 14-year-old retiree with one horn.

Paul transmits the "OK" signal back to Maximus Icon.

Immediately, the goat robot cries out, "HALT, GO DOUBLE TIME TO THE BACK OF THE HOUSE AND WAIT FOR FURTHER ORDERS." "DOUBLE TIME. HUP TWO THREE FOUR, HUP TWO THREE FOUR =========.

The midshipman takes off to the back of the house. The robot turns and hollers

"I'LL BE BACK" and then takes off while hitting his drums.

The next day a ransom note is found demanding that all NAVY cadets acknowledge that ARMY cadets are superior in any venture.

Within one day, both the Army and Naval Academies know about the theft. By the second day, the Maryland BroBible reads:

Maryland BroBible Headlines - "Army Cadets Kidnap, The Wrong Goat While Trying To Play a Prank On Navy.

*

"The U.S. Military Academy and the U.S. Naval Academy are disappointed by the trust that was broken recently between our brothers and sisters in arms. These actions do not reflect either academy's core values of dignity and respect," read a statement attributed to superintendents Lt. Gen Riddick and Vice Adm Swelch.

Although America's game does not kickoff for a few more weeks, Army is getting ahead of its rivalry with the Navy. However, the West Point cadets failed miserably and kidnapped the wrong goat.

After three days, Bill 34 was returned with the words "Sink the Navy" painted on its fur. No one mentions it. Bill No. 37 was in the corner of the barn snickering at the failed attempt. At least, that is what I was told.

Sharing their headline is another topic that is not so peaceful.

"Operation Desert Shield."

The New York papers headline read, **"Operation Desert Shield.** There is no mention of the attempt to take the Naval academy goat.

Peace reigns until the Fall of 1990.

The Naval Academy at Annapolis 1990

Naval Midshipmen are marching to the music of George Bernard Shaw's "Washington Post." column after column of midshipmen march in precise cadence past the reviewing stand. The last squad is 10 rows by 10 columns. Each of them carries an American flag on a pole. The midshipmen halt in front of the reviewing stand and perform a precision drill routine. At the end of each command, there is a loud symbol crash.

On the third sound of the symbols, the cadets rotate and replace the pole flags with a large American flag. Another symbol clashes and the large flag is popped. One more crash of the symbols, the large flag is then folded, and another crash and

"COMMANDER IN CHIEF," trophy is applauded by Navel Brass.

Officers, parents, and friends applauded. The music resumes, and the midshipmen march with the CIC to the Rotunda of Bancroft Hall.

Two hundred yards beyond the reviewing stand, the streets are ripped up, and water pipes are scattered about. In spite of the construction, most of the crowd walks to Bancroft Hall for the presentation of the "Commander-In-Chief (**CIC)** trophy.

Admiral Riddick is talking to one of the proud parents. "This is a great moment. We finally completed the modifications to Bancroft Hall, making it worthy of housing the CIC trophy." "What is the CIC?" the parent responds. "You will find out as soon as we get there." They continue walking casually and observe the construction. The noise of the equipment starting up is deafening. After a few minutes of walking, the crowd arrives at Bancroft Hall.

The CIC trophy is paraded into Bancroft Hall and placed on a pedestal in the Rotunda.

Commander Dolin will make the presentation of the trophy to the large crowd gathered in the Rotunda.

Commander Dolin: "Ladies and gentlemen, honored guests, and fellow officers. "In *1972, The* CIC *TROPHY was established in honor of the president. It is awarded to the academy that demonstrates academic and athletic supremacy for the previous year. During the years 1972 through 1990, the ARMY has held THE CIC TROPHY 5 times, the AIR FORCE 6 times, the NAVY 5 times, and THE CIC TROPHY has been shared four times. It is a three-sided structure, which weighs 270 lb. and stands 2 1/2 feet tall, is engraved with the seal of each academy, and displays a reproduction of each school's mascot. The year in which the trophy is won is engraved on the appropriate academy side. To the cadets of the military academies, (THE CIC TROPHY) is the World Series, the Super Bowl, Wimbledon, the World Cup, and the Olympics all rolled in one. To desecrate THE CIC TROPHY is unthinkable. The Academy that holds THE CIC TROPHY has immense bragging rights over the other academy's cadets. The Trophy is placed on a pedestal that is covered with glass. At night, the pedestal is lowered 20 feet into the ground. Electronic surveillance protects all entrances to the Rotunda; the CIC trophy must be protected, not from regular thieves, but from the other academies, especially ARMY.*"

The audience laughs.

Commander Dolin keys in a password. A humming sound attracts everyone's attention. The pedestal in the middle of the Rotunda comes alive with lights and sounds. The golden metal door on top of the pedestal opens. The CIC is placed on a pedestal. The cadet band starts to play

"The Liberty Bell March" by John Phillip Sousa.

The Commander-In-Chief Trophy

After refreshments and small talk, the crowd disperses, and only Admiral Riddick and Commander Dolin are present.

Admiral Riddick -. "Are you certain about this security system? Remember last year Army stole one of the mascots, but it was the wrong goat." They both laugh. "We have to be diligent. They may try again."

Commander Dolin and Admiral Riddick walk slowly to a panel at the door. Commander Dolin starts pressing codes to activate the security."

He enters the password for Heat Sensors. "HEAT SENSORS READY FOR ACTIVATION" blares out over the PA system.

He enters the password for Motion Sensors. "MOTION SENSORS READY FOR ACTIVATION" blares out over the PA system.

He enters the password for Sound Sensors. "SOUND SENSORS READY FOR ACTIVATION" blares out over the PA system.

He enters the password for Door Locks. "DOOR LOCKS READY FOR ACTIVATION."

He enters the password for Pedestal Sensors. "PEDESTAL SENSORS READY FOR ACTIVATION" blares out over the PA system.

Admiral Riddick and Commander Dolin walk out of the room. "30 SECONDS 20 SECONDS" ------ 10 SECONDS" ------

He turns around and gives one quick glance through the bulletproof window in the door.

"5 SECONDS," "4 SECONDS," "3 SECONDS," 2 SECONDS," 1 SECOND," "ACTIVATED. "

The ring of lights surrounding the pedestal turns off. The Glass enclosure clicks shut, and the trophy descends into its 20 ft grave.

The security devices click as they pulse their way back and forth across the dark and empty room. The sounds were given the nickname *"The ghost of the tap dancer."*

The CIC trophy is now all alone, as was the Navy goat, Bill, in 1955.

Fall 1990 – The Front-Line Bar

The "FRONT LINE" is one of many hangouts that cater to the Army cadets in their off time. The lounge is filled with cadets and local women wanting to latch on to a future officer. The walls of this rustic bar are covered with pictures of famous military leaders, cadet sporting events, and other nostalgic memories. Unfortunately, some cadets spend more free time on the "Front Line" than with their studies. The bartender "PINKY" has owned the bar since 1950. He gained his nickname while he was in action at the end of World War II in the battle of the Bulge. His unit was engaged in 20-degree weather for 6 days, during which both of his pinky fingers suffered serious frostbite and were amputated.

One of our heroes, P.M. Porto, enters the "Front Line." He immediately goes to the special Juke Box containing old Rock and Roll songs. He presses "C5." "THE BIRD. "As the song begins, he starts to dance and is immediately joined by Sesay Swift and John Little. The three friends perfectly imitate the Morris Day routine. As the song ends, they make their way back to the booth where <u>Maximus Icon</u> and <u>Chris Higginbottom</u> greet them.

They were celebrating their upcoming graduation in 1991. Discreetly they discuss their accomplishments during their stay at West Point and bemoan the fact that last year, they stole the wrong goat. The discussion gradually leads to the conclusion that they have to do something spectacular to make up for last year's blunder.

As they continue their discussion, <u>Chris Higginbottom</u> has attached 10 straws together and is unsuccessfully attempting to suck the liquid from a soft drink bottle. As he is about to attempt the 10-straw suck, Paul Toscano walks to the booth and inquires as to what Chris is trying to do. He is loud in his remarks. He questions the sanity of trying something so foolish and challenges Chris to a $25 wager. If Chris can attach 15 straws and successfully suck all the liquid from a soft drink bottle, Paul will give him the $25. Otherwise, Chris will give Paul $25. Chris declines, but John Little responds, "Chris, I'll pay if you lose." Chris says, "OK."

Paul Toscano asks if anybody else wants to bet against him. Some senior cadets in other booths shake their heads and turn away, but three freshman cadets jump at the chance to make an easy $25. John Little holds all the money for the challenge.

Apprehensively, Chris attaches 5 more straws and places one end into the soft drink bottle. The tension builds, and then the liquid starts to flow. Slowly at first, then faster and faster. Before anyone could say "SUCKER," the bottle was empty.

Sesay mummers, "Very Appropriate."

The freshman cadets started to protest, but when John Little did not protest, they calmed down. John then hands the money to Paul Toscano, who was invited to sit at their booth. Little did the freshman cadets know that they had been had. Paul and his companions had pulled this trick at least once a month for the last three years with uncanny success.

After congratulating themselves, Paul pulls out the evening paper. A second-page article reads
"Navy retains the Commander In Chief Trophy."

Paul leans toward the center of the table. The others also lean in.

"Gentlemen, are you interested"?

As the discussion begins, it might be helpful to know the background of our heroes.

The Cadets

CADET1 - **Paul Toscano** Is 6'2" 220lbs. He grew up in New Orleans and is a graduate of La Salle High School, also in New Orleans. He is an "A" student and has sports letters in Football, Tennis, Baseball, and Basketball. He is very sure of himself. He is the leader of the group and is a master of planning. His current cadet rank is Brigade Command Sergeant. He wants to make up for last year's attempt to steal the Navy goat. His eyes are on the CIC Trophy at Annapolis.

CADET2 – **John Little** – Is 6'4", 240lbs of solid muscle. Intellectual, Weight Lifter, Martial Arts, and Wrestler. He speaks like a Harvard professor. His main goal in life is to be a teacher. On the surface, he is mild and soft-spoken. He is basically against violence.

CADET3 – **Maximus Icon** – 5' 5" ,165lbs. Grew up in New York. Very smart. Super Computer Hacker, Communication Guru, Super Mechanic. He is a master of modifying electronic devices, a designer of robots, and an expert programmer. He grew up near West Point and had many technical contacts in the area.

CADET4 - **P.M. Porto** – 5' 11" ,220lbs. High School Track Star. He won the Louisiana State 400-meter dash. His father was born in Kuwait. He speaks the Arabic and Kurdish languages. He moved to New Orleans when he was eight. In the 14 years that he lived in New Orleans, he called it " New Awlins," he talked like a local.

CADET5 - **Sesay Swift** – 5'5" 150lbs; Funny Guy – His humor is dry and somewhat sarcastic. He very seldom gets flustered except when he is.

CADET6 - **Chris Higginbottom** – 5'5" 160lbs. Very nervous. Has the best intentions but usually blunders whatever he is doing? His second cousin on his mother's side is Don Knotts. His nickname is "Bumbler." Loveable and loyal.

Paul Toscano is discussing the CIC trophy with his fellow cadets. His discussion emphasizes the following.

1 Last year we messed up. We should have done more investigation before attempting to take the Navy goat. We would have known that there were about 15 of them and that the lights would be turned off, making it even more difficult to take the right goat.

2 Security at the goat barn is better than Fort Knox since our mess-up last year. They have installed cameras and two guards.

3 Nobody is even thinking about stealing the CIC trophy. That's a plus in our favor.

4 The CIC trophy weighs 270 lbs. It's awkward to transport. We have to figure out a way to move the trophy without damaging it.

5 The CIC is protected by its location in the rotunda at Bancroft Hall at the Naval Academy.

6 The CIC is protected by five "state of the art" security systems in the rotunda. Right now, we don't have any idea how they work,

7 The CIC is locked in a cylinder 20 feet down in the ground.

8 The streets around Bancroft Hall are all torn up with construction work, making it almost impossible to get a truck close to it.

9 If we are caught, it means expulsion and possible jail time.

They look at each other with dead stares.

THEN

"Sesay Swift" "Soooo What's the problem?

As they continue the discussion, their voices get louder. This attracts the attention of cadet Reginald Wadsworth in the next booth.

Reginald Wadsworth (6'2", 200 lbs.) is a junior cadet at the army academy; His father is a US representative from Maine. He is the second-string QB on the football team. He wants to raise his status at the academy. As a platoon sergeant, he knows how to control men under his command. He has six loyal cadets that are also football players.

Reginal is listening as Paul discusses the plan.

The discussion ends with, **"Should we try it or leave well enough alone. Should we jeopardize our graduation for the sake of one more time?"**

They go silent. Then after a pause, Paul Toscano places his hand in the middle of the table. One by the others file suit.

They decide to do it.

Reginald Wadsworth frowns. The noise of the barroom prevents him from hearing anymore.

As Paul's group gets up to leave, P.M. Porto goes to the Juke Box and presses "C9."

"JUNGLE LOVE. "Everybody jumps to the dance floor and starts singing and dancing. "Ohhhh - O --- O- E- O- E- O"

Everybody is dancing.

FIRST TRIP TO BANCROFT HALL

Early Fall 1990. 6:00 AM

Navy Commander Dolin enjoys the serenity of the Navel campus as he walks toward Bancroft Hall. He knows that at 7:00 AM, the city workers will crank up their machinery, and it will continue until 20:00 (8:00 PM). As he unlocks the doors and disarms the security systems, he looks with pride at the pedestal in the center of the room. He enters the passwords, and the CIC is rising from its 20' tomb. When it reaches the surface, the metal casing opens, and there is the CIC in all its splendor.

7:00 AM

At the same time as the CIC trophy is rising, Paul Toscano and Maximus Icon get off of a bus at the NAVY academy. They are dressed in civilian clothes. They proceed to walk in the direction of Bancroft Hall.

Bancroft Hall

Maximus Icon is sitting in the first row in the center of the photo wearing a light blue shirt. Paul Toscano is in a yellow shirt. He is walking up the right ramp of Bancroft Hall.

There is heavy road construction in progress.

City workers are like ants digging up sections of the street and putting down the new pipe. The foreman is wearing a sleeveless jacket. He is about 54 years old. They ask him what's going on. He told them that the water and sewerage lines were being replaced. They asked for directions to the Bancroft Hall, where the CIC is displayed. The city worker explodes. His veins in his neck were about to burst. He hates the Navy. After ranting, he finally calms down. "Sorry about that; I'm Frank Bluster, an old ARMY guy and the foreman of this job. Bancroft Hall is right over there. His tattoo clearly displays "ARMY" on his 18" bicep as he extends his arm in the direction of Bancroft Hall.

As the cadets start to walk towards Bancroft Hall. All of a sudden, DEAD SILENCE.

All electrical equipment stops. The foreman snickers. "Every now and then, we have to cut off the electricity for about 4 minutes to switch power sources. It gives the security guys fits. We are using as much power on this job as was used to build the entire academy."

As Paul and Maximus walk to the rotunda, they too are captured by the beauty and serenity of the campus. At Bancroft Hall, they make a note of the beauty of the rotunda. One by one, they study the five security devices, especially the pillar in the center of the room. The room can hold over 200 people. The open space makes detection easy. They need a way to disable not just one but five systems before they are detected. They can use the 4 minutes of no power. The only way that it can be done is if we turn off the electricity. A big smile is on Maximus's Face. He looks at Paul and whispers - "They have the name of the company that installed the security equipment. "Maximus knows this company ("Dewey, Cheatem, and Howe" an alarm company. They have offices all over the country. Their office in New York is only a few miles from West Point. "What a break." "Let's get back to the dorm.

Later that evening, Maximus Icon is on the INTERNET. He Google Searches for (Dewey, Cheatem, and Howe). He gathers information on the type of alarm systems they support and matches them against the systems found in Bancroft Hall. This is like finding the Rosetta Stone.

From his experience, Maximus Icon knows that he must make personal contact with someone at their New York office. He comes up with a plan. The next morning, he travels to the New York Office of ("Dewey, Cheatem, and Howe") and becomes friends with one of the employees. Without identifying himself as an army cadet, he obtains enough information to disable the security systems.

The security system is a dual modular relay. The on-site processing unit uses the time of day to program the sensors. During the day, most of the sensors are turned off, except for the video cameras and the sensor protecting the CIC trophy (it is always on). At night, five sensors are set. The on-site processing unit then monitors the sensors and relays the information back to the central office ("Dewey, Cheatem, and Howe") and to the Naval Security office at the academy.

The problem is that they only have 4 minutes to replace the modules. Any longer than that will raise the suspicions of the on-site security.

Maximus Icon decides he will construct two electronic devices. One will be inserted between the on-site processing unit and the sensors, and the other one will be inserted between the on-site processing unit and the central office. The plan is simple; one unit will tell the sensors that everything is normal. The other unit will intercept the real information from the on-site unit and tell the main office that everything is OK. Maximus needs 4 minutes of tape without activity. The 4-minute video will be transmitted to the Naval security office and to the alarm company. He can do this when the electricity is shut off for 4 minutes. When the electricity is turned back on at Bancroft Hall, the Alarm Company will think that the power was turned off because of the construction and reset the recording times froward 4 minutes. Little do ("Dewey, Cheatem, and Howe") know, but they are part of the equation for covering up the theft.

Paul agrees with the plan.

Later at the "FRONT-LINE."

Maximus Icon arrives late at the "FRONT-LINE" and immediately starts talking about the plan. Paul Toscano will cut off the electricity. Maximus Icon and Chris Higginbottom will enter the tundra and install the modules. Sesay Swift, John Little, and P.M. Porto will get the CIC. *(Make sure that the pedestal is all the way up before removing the CIC. Whatever they do, they must not remove the CIC before it stops moving.)*

The rear door of the hall offers the best cover and the easiest route of entry and escape. The plan is foolproof, or so it may seem. Unbeknown to our heroes, Reginald Wadsworth, and his buddies are in the next booth and overhear part of the plan. Between the noise and the music, Reginald hears "last year's mistake" and later, "it's well protected."

■■

What does it all mean?

Reginald has long suspected Paul of stealing the navy goat but could not prove it.

Reginald sees Chris Higginbottom writing a few notes. When Chris prepares to leave the booth, he drops the paper on the floor. Reginald Wadsworth picks up the note, unseen by anyone. The note reads, "Bancroft Hall tomorrow 9:00 AM."

THE SECOND TRIP TO ANNAPOLIS

At 9:00 AM the next morning, our six cadets dressed in civilian clothes get off the train at the Naval academy. They spot the foreman. Paul establishes that he is a DIE-HARD Army man. He hates the NAVY. He goes by the nickname of "Phineas."

Our heroes then proceed to Bancroft Hall and make notes of what they see. They then discuss if it is worth it to risk their military careers for one more steal.

From a safe distance, Reginald Wadsworth is watching. He sees our cadets leave the crane operator and walk towards Bancroft Hall. After an hour, they leave the Hall, and Reginald goes in. He immediately spots the "Commander-In-Chief trophy."

Then it comes to him. Last year, whoever stole the Navy goat, stole the wrong one, and they want to do something better. It confirms Reginald's suspicion that Paul Toscano was involved. But, if he is going to steal something more exciting than the Navy goat, what could it be? He fixates on the CIC trophy, "No, not that." Then he begins to laugh.

Commander Dolin observes Reginald's behavior and gets suspicious. He notes the time and walks to a small room with a PC. He opens an app that displays the security tape. He enters the time. The tape stops with a clear image of Reginald Wadsworth. He passes the image to the Naval student security to confirm the picture.

The reply is:

"No visual, 20-22 years old, Military haircut, not a Naval academy student."

Commander Dolin backups the tape for 1 hour and starts scrutinizing every frame. He notices some young men are intensely looking at the security systems. He takes pictures of the young men and passes their images to the Naval student security system.

He gets the following 6 responses.

"No visual, 20-22 years old, Military haircut, not a Naval academy student."

"No visual, 20-22 years old, Military haircut, not a Naval academy student."

"No visual, 20-22 years old, Military haircut, not a Naval academy student."

"No visual, 20-22 years old, Military haircut, not a Naval academy student."

"No visual, 20-22 years old, Military haircut, not a Naval academy student."

"No visual, 20-22 years old, Military haircut, not a Naval academy student."

Commander Dolin is puzzled.

"Seven young men on campus. None of them is a student. Interested in security systems.

He calls Captain Charles Simms De Witt at West Point. "I am going to send you some pictures. Can you pass them through your student security system and let me know if you know them?"

"OK," Captain De Witt responds.

After a few minutes, the seven pictures come across. He passes them through the student security system with the following results.

Picture 1 – Senior Paul Toscano

Picture 2 – Senior John Little

Picture 3 – Senior Maximus Icon

Picture 4 – Senior P.M. Porto

Picture 5 – Senior Sesay Swift

Picture 6 – Senior Chris Higginbottom

Picture 7 - Junior Reginald Wadsworth

"Commander Dolin, this is Captain De Witt. All seven of the young men are West Point cadets. Is there a problem"?

"NO, but it is strange that 7 of your cadets would be interested in the security systems at Bancroft Hall at the same time. Are they working on some project?"

De Witt - "None that I'm aware of. Is there anything else that I can help you with?"

Commander Dolin - "No Thanks."

Captain De Witt - "OK Then, Bye."

Something is brewing

ASSISTANT COMMANDER. (Captain Charles Simms De Witt), the Army Academy's new assistant commander walks towards General E.G. Yager's office.

De Witt's father was a Senator. His grandfather was a Colonel in World War II. His goal is to be a General, no matter how many people he has to step on. He is a "BY THE BOOK" commander.

COMMANDANT: (General E.G. Yager), A grassroots country boy who rose through the ranks by his accomplishments. Great common sense. Trustworthy. Good listener. Never speaks until he has all the facts. Makes good decisions.

A plaque on his desk reads:

"A spirit mission, gentlemen, is an activity undertaken by cadets that are typically somewhat against regulations yet demonstrate qualities that the academy supposedly seeks to develop: audacity, teamwork, creativity, and mission focus. The successful accomplishment of a good spirit mission enhances the spirit not only of the cadets involved but also that of the whole Corps and the greater West Point community in general"

- "Spirit Mission," a novel by Ted Russ

The two officers discuss what reason could bring 7 cadets to Bancroft Hall at Annapolis at the same time? De Witt continues, "Isn't it almost time for the annual football game?" "Yes," he answers General Yager. De Witt jumps to a conclusion. "They are going to steal the Navy goat."

"General Yager" - "At Bancroft Hall?"

General Yager becomes silent but is thinking. 'The goat is out of the question with last year's mess-up. They will have all the goats doubly protected. Especially after **"I'll be back"** was painted on the back of one of the goats last year. "No. it must be something else."

General Yager - "Call Commander Dolin and tell him that we are not aware of any problems with the seven cadets, but remember that we both have to be on alert as the Big Game gets closer."

AT THE FRONT-LINE

"At the FRONT-LINE LOUNGE" the night before the steal.

Our heroes are discussing the final details and setting a date for tomorrow night.

Reginald Wadsworth overhears the conversation. He has his own plan. His men will stay behind Paul's men. Reginald's men are bigger. Whatever Paul's men take from Bancroft Hall, his men will take it away from them. If Paul's men fail, his men will disappear into the background uncaught.

"SMART and SIMPLE." "BRAWN OVER BRAIN. "

The phone rings, and Pinky answers. He shouts out, "Who's Paul. It's for you."

Paul picks up the phone, "Hello," He listens for a minute then hangs up, and leaves the lounge.

The Night of the Steal

The moon is bright on the night of the STEAL. Our heroes are at the rear of Bancroft Hall. They split up and then proceeded to put their plan into action. Paul Toscano maneuvers to the circuit breaker and turns the electricity off. The rest of the cadets enter the rear of the building and proceed to insert the reprogrammed modules into the alarm circuitry. Reginald Wadsworth and his cadets watch patiently from nearby bushes. At the end of four minutes, Paul Toscano turns on the electricity. The new modules kick in. (Show that the sensors are disarmed, that the locks unlock, and that the central office thinks that everything is OK). Paul's team then proceeds to the encasement of the CIC trophy and turns on the switch to bring it up from its 20' grave. As it starts to ascend, Reginald Wadsworth's cadets think that THE TROPHY has already been recovered. They turn off the lights and storm the building. During the scuffle, the glass cover of the vault is removed before the CIC pedestal reaches the top.

The alarm goes off.

Within a minute, Navy security arrives and captures everyone. Paul looks disgusted that everything went so wrong.

After a short wait, Commander Dolan arrives on the scene. He is very upset. His interrogation of the cadets reveals two separate intentions. One is to steal the CIC, and the second is to save the trophy. Commander Dolan emits a sarcastic laugh and then proceeds to the wall panel and enters the password that will raise the pedestal the remaining way. As they are lined up, the pedestal is opened.

Sesay – "**IT'S MISSING** !!!!!"

Someone throws a tennis ball at him.

All the cadets are at a loss. Nobody has the CIC. Captain De Witt is called to the scene. He threatens expulsion unless they tell him who has THE TROPHY. (NO ONE KNOWS).

The next morning Captain De Witt storms into General Yager's office. "We got the culprits." General Yager responds, "What culprits?"

De Witt – "The ones that stole the CIC trophy."

Yager's – "So that's what they were after. "Is it OK?"

De Witt – It's missing!

Yager – "What do you mean it's missing?

De Witt – "The Navel security guards arrested everybody while the heist was in progress, but the trophy was missing. Nobody knows where it is.

Yager - Then what was stolen? The trophy weighs over 270 pounds. No one person could easily carry it off through the busted streets. Have any trucks been near the rotunda?"

De Witt – "We do not know!"

The General nods. "Then, are you saying that the CIC could be in the building"? No response.

General Yager has become silent. He has something else on his mind.

"Captain, you are going to have to handle this problem by yourself. I've been transferred to Operation "Desert Storm." Something is going to begin soon. General Schwarzkoph has requested my services.

De Witt is ecstatic but hides his emotions. He extends his hand and gives General Yager a handshake, "Congratulations."

At last, he will preside over a court-martial as Judge.

The Hearing

Two weeks later, the court secretary opened the hearing. "ALL RISE. " This hearing will determine if the accused cadets will face Court Martial. Captain De Witt will be the presiding officer in place of General Yager, who has been reassigned to Iraq.

Captain De Witt takes his place on the stand and reads the charges. "On the night of September 2, 1990. Twelve West Point cadets participated in the break-in at the Bancroft Hall on the Naval Academy at Annapolis. As a result, the "Commander-In-Chief" trophy is missing, and there was damage done to the rotunda." This hearing will determine if there is sufficient evidence to proceed with a court-martial.

Who represents the plaintiff? Commander Dolin stands. "I Do "

Captain De Witt - "Are the charges as stated?"

Commander Dolin – "Yes"

Captain De Witt" – "Would you present your evidence."

Commander Dolin – "Start the Tape. Here we see six of the defendants casually walking through the rotunda in Bancroft Hall. Notice how much attention they give to the security systems. Then, after an hour, they leave. Within minutes from the time that the six cadets leave the rotunda, a single cadet, I believe to be Cadet Reginald Wadsworth, enters the rotunda. Notice how exuberant he is as he laughs before the CIC trophy.

De Witt – I see no crime here.

Dolin – No crime, but suspicions. Now let's look at the tape on the night of the theft."

Starting at 18:06, the security at tape shows 4 minutes of nothing." This is also is what Navy security sees."

De Witt – "This still shows nothing."

Dolin – Correct, but now, let's see what the recording in the rotunda sees at the same time. There 4 minutes are missing, then the lights go on, showing 12 cadets fighting, and the lights go off. You can hear the fighting but no video. Next, whistles are blowing, and the lights go on. All of the cadets are captured, and the trap doors on the pedestal are still locked. Commander Dolin enters the building, looks around, and walks to the pedestal. He is satisfied that the trap doors are still locked, laughs, and walks to the security panel. He keys in the pedestal password. The trap doors unlock and open. The sound of the rising platform is griping. **The trophy is not there**. Everybody is shocked.

Sesay can be heard saying, **"It's missing !!** Sesay turns to John Little, "I said that," "I said that," nodding his head.

De Witt – "Commander, I can see evidence for breaking and entry, but there is nothing I see that ties them to the theft of the CIC trophy. I can't even confirm that the trophy was in the tundra at the time of the break-in."

Captain De Witt's term as a court-martial judge has evaporated.

He retires to his office. The phone is ringing.

General Yager at the IRAQ Command Center

General Yager has been assigned to the Intelligence Unit. It comes to his attention that the IRAQ radar shield is vulnerable at a particular location North East of Arar.

Because of the terrain, there are two radar stations that are not overlapped by other stations. If these two stations can be knocked out, it will open a 25–30-mile pathway for the air force to enter IRAQ undetected.

The knockout can be done only by a small group of trained soldiers. They must be able to secretly enter Iraq, destroy the two sights, and get out without alarming the enemy. It gives us about two hours of undetected time to send bombers through to a target-rich environment.

General Yager recognizes that the cadets currently at the hearing have the talent for this type of assignment. He secretly admires their ability to plan and initiate detailed maneuvers and to improvise when required. He also knows that Captain De Witt wants to court-martial the cadets.

General Yager – "Sergeant, Get me Captain De Witt at West Point."

De Witt picks up the phone.

Yager - "Captain, how is the hearing coming?"

De Witt - "It's almost over, sir. We can court-martial them for damages and breaking and entry, but not for the theft of the CIF trophy."

Yager – "Don't be so hasty, Captain. I have a mission that requires their skills. Rather than court-martial and expel them, let's use their talents and energy. There are two opposing groups of cadets. Right?" "Yes, Sir."

Yager – "Good. Train them as separate Special Forces units and then have them compete. The winners will go to Iraq on a special mission, and the losers will resign.

This gives them the opportunity of helping their country or to quietly be dismissed. If they choose to go to IRAQ, they will be allowed to return to the ACADEMY and graduate.

Captain De Witt likes the idea. He will produce a skilled group of cadets and remove a less-than-perfect group. At the hearing, he renders his decision, "The cadets will train for Iraq."

Commander Dolin is not pleased.

The next morning the twelve cadets are given leave from the Academy. They pack their bags and fly to North Carolina.

Special Opts Training at Fort Bragg

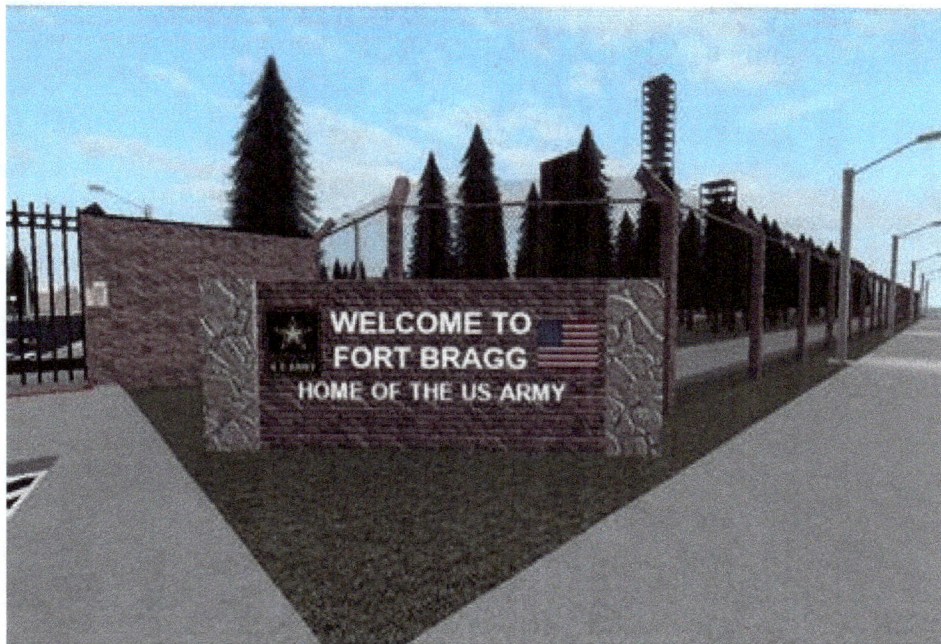

Upon arrival at Fort Bragg, they go directly to their assigned barracks and unload their duffel bags.

Sergeant Quizzo appears. "Atten... hup.

Line up outside in 2 rows. Paul Toscano's squad in row 1 and Reginald Wadsworth's squad in row 2.

......**Now!**"

After 15 seconds of mayhem, the cadets are in a single line.

Sergeant Quizzo – "Gentlemen, where is squad 2." The cadets scramble and correctly make 2 rows.

Sergeant Quizzo – "Very good. Right Face, Double time harsch."

For 30 minutes, they follow Sergeant Quizzo's commands. Finally, he shouts, "Ready ... halt. "

They are in front of their barracks again.

Sergeant Quizzo – "Go take a shower. Mess is at 18:00. Reveille is at 05:00 AM. **Dismissed**."

05:00 – The trumpet blares reveille. Sesay Swift jumps out of his bed and runs into a barracks column. **"Ohooooo,"** as he slumps to the floor.

At 05:30, Sergeant Quizzo appears outside of the barracks. "Atten… hup. Gentlemen. Go to mess. Cadet Toscano. As the highest-ranking cadet, you are in charge when I'm not around. Take your men to breakfast. Be back by 06:30."

Cadet Toscano takes charge and marches the men to the mess hall. At 06:15, he marches them back to the barracks.

At 06:30, Sergeant Quizzo appears outside of the barracks. "Atten… hup. Gentlemen, we are going to get the special equipment that has been assigned to you. Right Face, Double time harsch." Twenty minutes later, they are in line at the armory. Bags and bags of equipment are given to them.

Sesay Swift – "This looks like my momma at a Black Friday Sale." He loads up and goes outside. In twenty minutes, all of the cadets have their full load.

Sergeant Quizzo – "Gentlemen. Take care of this equipment. It may save your life. Each of you has manuals for the equipment you will use on your mission. You have 3 weeks to know everything. Rifles first."

Sergeant Quizzo – "Atten... hup. Left Face, ... harsch. Hup 1, Hup2, Hup3, ..."

Forty minutes later, they are at the barracks.

Sergeant Quizzo – "Gentlemen. Reveille is at 05:00. Be dressed in full combat gear. Use the rest of today to familiarize yourself with the compound. Lights out at 21.00".

Sergeant Quizzo leaves the barracks. The cadets start unpacking.

Sesay Swift – "How did we get into this predicament?" Someone throws a tennis ball hat at him.

At 04:00, Sergeant Quizzo appears in the barracks. "Atten Hut. Gentlemen. Assemble outside in full combat gear. Be ready at 05:00."

It's 04:50. The cadets are outside of their barracks.

Chris Higginbottom – "I thought reveille was at 05:00?"

Sesay Swift – "It is. We're early so we can wake up the bugler."

Sergeant Quizzo appears – "Gentlemen "Atten... hup. Right Face, Forwardddd Harsch Hup 1, Hup 2, ...

After running for 30 minutes in full gear, they arrive at the mess hall and take their breakfast in full gear as if they were in field combat.

Sergeant Quizzo – appears. "Gentlemen, this is your last meal at the mess hall. You are in combat. You will prepare meals as if you were in the field. You will study in the field. You will sleep in the field. Every third day you will receive supplies just as if you were in combat. Be ready at 07:00."

The men struggle to sit on the chairs in the mess hall while wearing their equipment.

As they try to take off their equipment, an old burly (sergeant) cook comes up to them. "Don't drop your stuff on my floor. Go Outside."

They mumble as they walk out. Chris Higginbottom trips, and Sesay Swift walks on him and over him. Chris groans. "Ooooohoho." John Little picks up Chris and all of his equipment.

John Little - "Come on, Tarzan."

At 07:00, Sergeant Quizzo appears. "Atten... hup. Right Face, Double time harsch." They run for 10 minutes to the rifle range. There, they learn to operate their special equipment and fire their rifles. All of them have rifle experience from the academy. They are still mumbling about having to eat outside with their equipment. Afterward, they are allowed to rest outside the barracks.

Sesay looks at all of his equipment and mumbles. "This is heavier than me." Referring to his Duffle bag.

13:00 - Sergeant Quizzo appears and bellows. "Atten Hut," "Right Face," Double Time Harsch" hup two three, four, hup ...."

Sesay sounds like a junk man as they runoff.

Ten minutes later, they are at the parachute launch site.

Sergeant Quizzo – "Gentlemen, today, you will learn to jump using conventional parachutes. We will practice until dark. When you parachute in Iraq, the conditions will be similar to what you see now."

Sesay's First Jump.

They start off with the jump and roll as they hit the ground. Next, they load some of their equipment and practice jumps and rolls. Finally, they load all of their equipment, including ammunition and explosives.

Sesay hits the ground, and his duffle bag explodes. It is a small explosive that was placed by Sergeant Quizzo to teach them how to pack the explosives and how to land.

He goes to Paul Toscano's duffle bag and removes the explosive.

Sesay to Paul - "You must have maid service."

The cadets practice as it gets dark.

The sun has long set as they arrive at the barracks.

Sergeant Quizzo appears. "Atten Hut. Gentlemen, you are under field conditions. Remove your food from your duffle bags and select what you want to eat. You have 20 minutes. Remember to clean your utensils. Repack your duffel bag.

They scramble for their food. The sound is very loud.

After eating and repacking, most duffel bags look larger than before they ate, Sesay's bag is as long as he is tall. "Whatttttt," John Little's bag looks extra light.

Sergeant Quizzo bellows. "Atten Hut, Gentlemen, you are in combat. Take your sleeping bag out of your duffle bag. You can sleep anywhere on this lawn. Lights out at 20:00. Reveille is tomorrow at 05:00. "Goodnight, gentlemen."

Reginald Wadsworth goes over to Paul Toscano. "Paul, can I see you a second?"

They walk a few steps outside of the lawn area.

Reginald Wadsworth – "Paul, we don't have to be here. You know that my father is a U.S. senator. He will pull some strings, and this will all be erased from our records. I want to make you a deal. If you tell me where the CID is, I will see to it that my father takes care of you."

Paul – "Listen, scumbag. It's because of you that we are in this mess. I'll take my chances alone. Get out of my sight if you don't want your pretty face messed up."

For the next 14 days, the practice routine is repeated until they can use their equipment in their sleep. On the 15th day at 5:00 AM, Sergeant Quizzo appears. "Atten… hup. Right Face, Double time harsch." After 30 minutes, they are at the rifle range.

06:00 Sergeant Quizzo – "Today, you will separate into two teams.

Team 1 is Paul Toscano's cadets. Team 2 is Reginald Wadsworth's cadets. Each team will be graded on their ability to shoot and use explosives effectively. Each cadet will fire 5 shots at the 200-yard target."

All of the cadet's shoot and their targets are graded. **It's a tie.**

It's 10:00 AM. Sergeant Quizzo appears. "Atten... hup. Right Face, Double time harsch." Twenty minutes later, they approach an area that is like another world. It looks barren. Few trees, shrubs, and straw weeds.

Sergeant Quizzo "Gentleman, we are going to test your camouflage ability. You may use anything you have in your duffle bag to assist you. You have 20 minutes to hide yourself and your equipment. My staff and I will hunt you out. If you remain hidden for more than 1 hour, you win."

All of the cadets go to their duffle bags and grab shovels, clothes, and anything that can be useful. After 20 minutes, no one can be seen.

Sergeant Quizzo and his staff start searching. Three of Reginald Wadsworth's squad are hidden under a thick bush. They cannot be seen, but with every breath, the bush shakes. They are found immediately. John Little's large frame is hard to cover. He lays on his back, but his right shoe is sticking out of the sand. He's found. Maximus Icon finds a small cave. He climbs into the cave and puts rocks to cover the entry. Unfortunately, he leaves his helmet on the cave entry. He's found.

One by one, Sergeant Quizzo and his staff find the other hidden cadets. Some they step on, some they yank out of the sand, some they pull straws out of the cadet's mouth, some they poke with a stick.

At the end of the hour, only 2 cadets are still hidden. Paul Toscano and Chris Higginbottom. Sergeant Quizzo gets on his microphone. "Will the remaining cadets come up from their camouflage position? Paul Toscano comes up between two of the staff members.

Sergeant Quizzo – "Well done." There is no sign of Chris Higginbottom. Sergeant Quizzo calls again. Everybody is looking. Still nothing. Sergeant Quizzo gets the Bull horn, he puts it on full volume, and screams – "Higginbottom" – "Higginbottom" – "Higginbottom." Finally, one of the cadets sees some movement in the sand. A reed is moving without the wind. Sergeant Quizzo goes to the spot and delicately lowers his hand, and pulls gently on the reed. It comes out of the ground but is connected to a horizontal reed. Gently he lifts the reed, which is 5' long and connected to another horizontal reed. Finally, he feels a piece of cloth. He gently lifts the cloth and sees Higginbottom. He is sleeping with a reed in his mouth. He is rudely awakened and dragged to the road.

Sergeant Quizzo marks his book. <u>One tie and one win for Paul Toscano's team.</u>

"Gentlemen. Tonight, we will eat and sleep right here. Revelry arrives very fast, so sleep well." He laughs.

The cadets are dead tired. There is a little small talk that fades into silence.

Sesay Swift has set up his sleeping bag under a stack of wood. He zips up his sleeping bag and goes gently to sleep.

The bugler blares his trumpet at 05:00. The Army even has sound systems in the fields. Sesay jumps up and hits his head on a large board while still inside the bag. He sinks back to the ground with a sorrowful groan.

At 5:30, Sergeant Quizzo appears. "Atten… hup. Right Face HOLD IT." He walks over to Sesay. "WHAT HAPPENED TO YOU?" Sesay looks like he has sprouted a horn. He cannot put on his helmet.

Sergeant Quizzo – "Go to sickbay and get some ice on it. Come back as soon as the doctors let you." Sesay heads off to the infirmary.

Sergeant Quizzo "Gentleman, we are going to teach you how to use our communication equipment not only to communicate but also how to set off explosives and to direct something called LASER /GPS bombs to their targets. Right Face, Double time harsch."

Twenty minutes later, they approach the technical building. They go to Room T2. Each student takes a desk. Paul's group is on the left, and Reginald Wadsworth's group is on the right.

The instructor enters the room. "Sergeant Tivoli." Good morning, men. Before you are many types of explosives and detonators. Many different things to learn and many things that can mess up. But suppose we could have any of these explosives detonated under different circumstances by a single detonator and then transmit the results immediately back to the command center.

"In the past, we needed a special detonator for each explosive. Now we can attach a single detonator to any of these explosives and program it to explode under specific conditions. Gentlemen meet the 'Chameleon.'"

This device can be programmed to activate under the following parameters:

TIME DELAY, TIME OF DAY, HEAT, COLD, PRESSURE, FLAME, SMOKE, DISTANCE, SPEED, REPETITIONS, AND ROTATION.

Sergeant Tivoli- "Each team will be given 10 Chameleons. You have 48 hours from 15:00 to program your Chameleon to activate under each set of conditions. When you are finished, give me the settings for each of your Chameleon settings."

Programming The Chameleon

Maximus Icon's eyes light up. He lives for something like this to happen.

The Chameleon is a 4" black cube with dials and switches on 5 of the 6 sides and a ½" hole on the 6th side.

"Maximus – "This is a programable switch. Instead of an ON/OFF switch, it is a programable switch. When the program is satisfied, whatever has been inserted in the ½" hole is activated.

Example: If the Chameleon is programmed to activate when the TIME is 18:00, and a blasting cap is inserted into the hole, it will explode at exactly 18:00.

If the radio were inserted into the hole, the radio would go on at 18:00.

If a transmitter were inserted into the hole, it would send signals starting at 18:00.

The manual is simple for Maximus to digest. He doesn't need 2 days to learn it. He finishes the programs for each of the Chameleon in only 6 hours. He's ready.

Sergeant Tivoli is impressed. He looks at the individual program settings on each of Maximus's Chameleons. The basic settings are correct. He will not kill himself. Sergeant Tivoli places each Chameleon and its settings in the closet, close the door and locks it.

The next two days fly by for Reginald Wadsworth's team. They have worked throughout the night. As they approach the 48th hour, panic starts to set in. They have not figured out how to set the parameters for the ROTATION activation.

They <u>have dial "L3" set to 16</u>. This is not an illegal setting, but it will prevent the Chameleon from activating. Sergeant Tivoli checks the settings. They are "OKAY." He opened the closet. Reginald starts to place his Chameleon in the closet. He notices which of Maximus Icon's Chameleon is set for ROTATION. As Reginald starts to put his ROTATION Chameleon on the shelf, he distracts Sergeant Tivoli by asking him for a napkin to wipe off some grease. When Sergeant Tivoli turns and grabs the napkin, Reginald switches the Chameleons. Sergeant Tivoli gives Reginald the napkin and continues to watch the detonators.

Sergeant Tivoli leaves.

At 15:00, Sergeant Quizzo appears. "Gentlemen, let's see what you have learned about the Chameleon.

Under field conditions, we would have inserted blasting caps into the hole in the Chameleon, but tonight, we will use electric buzzers instead of blasting caps.

The judges have lined up your Chameleons in the following order.

 1 TIME, 2 HEAT, 3 COLD, 4 PRESSURE, 5 FLAME,6 SMOKE,7 DISTANCE,

 8 SPEED, 9 REPETIONS,10 ROTATION

Paul Toscano's team brings up the Chameleon set for TIME activation after 3 seconds. Maximus Icon looks at the programmed settings. They are as he set them.

 Sargant Tivoli – "ACTIVAT". One, Two, three … Bzzzzzzz

Reginald Wadsworth brings up his TIME detonator.

Sergeant Tivoli – "Are the settings correct?" Reginald has no clue, but he answers, "Yes, Sir." It's impressive."

Sargeant Tivoli – "ACTIVATE "After a 3-second delay, "Bzzzzzzz."

The next test is the HEAT Chameleon. Each team successfully activates its Chameleon. All activations are successful as we reach the last tests. "ROTATION. " As Maximus retrieves it. He notices that the "L3" dial is set to 16. He calls Sergeant Tivoli. "Sergeant, a parameter has been changed since last night." Tivoli looks at the detonator.

"Sorry, nothing can be modified."

Maximus places the ROTATION Chameleon on a 5-foot concrete ramp. Then, he inserts a buzzer into the hole.

Sargant Tivoli – "ACTIVAT".

A pendulum swings and hits the Chameleon. It begins to roll down the ramp. "One, TWO, THREE, FOUR rotations ... "NOTHING." The CHAMELEON is picked up by a robot, and the buzzer is removed.

Sargent Tivoli – "TRY AGAIN WITH A DIFFERENT BUZZER"

Maximus reruns the test, and "NOTHING."

Maximus has not been looking at the Chameleon. His attention has been directed at Reginald Wadsworth. Wadsworth is smiling and whispering.

Sergeant Tivoli "Sorry, cadet Icon. Your test is marked as a failure. Cadet Wadsworth, your turn."

Reginald Wadsworth picks up his Chameleon and sarcastically addresses Paul's group. "Second string. You had your chance. Now watch the big boys."

HE sets up his Chameleon on the concrete ramp.

Sargant Tivoli – "ACTIVAT"

The pendulum hits the Chameleon. It begins to roll down the ramp. "One, TWO, THREE, FOUR rotations   …   Bzzzzzzzz"

Reginald Wadsworth jumps and hollers. Maximus Icon is upset. He runs to Sergeant Quizzo, "Sergeant –"` Somebody changed the settings on my detonator. Wadsworth butts in "Sore loser." Maximus sprints at Reginald, but John Littles grabs him. There is a lot of shoving and pushing.

Sergeant Quizzo has had enough. . "Atten… hup. Everybody over there except cadets Icon and Wadsworth. Sergeant Tivoli, please bring me the cards with the detonator settings."

He looks over the cards and turns to the two cadets. "You have 1 minute to write down the settings of the ROTATION Chameleon.". Cadet Maximus Icon finishes in 15 seconds. Cadet Reginald Wadsworth takes the full minute. He looks up sheepishly. "Better to be safe than sorry."

Sargeant Quizzo – "Cadet Icon, the settings you wrote down were not the setting that was on your detonator. You wrote down the correct setting of 23, but your detonator was set to 16. Cadet Wadsworth, you wrote down 16, but your detonator setting was set to 23,

There is dead silence. Sergeant Reginald Wadsworth – "I screwed up." He and Sergeant Quizzo leave the area.

The next morning at 05:00 reveille. Sergeant Quizzo appears. "Atten… hup."

Only Paul Toscano's squad is in formation.

SPECIAL TRAINING WITH THE PARA-GLIDER

A truck pulls up to the armory and drops off some bundles containing Para-Gliders. The Para-Glider is the latest in gliders technology. It can glide miles without any wind. Their training continues with hand-to-hand combat, camouflage training, explosives, and jumps with the "Para-Glider." The training is being rushed. Activity at Fort Bragg is in full gear. The final practice with the new para-glider. Has gone extremely well.

JAN 10, 1991

The night before our cadets leave for Saudi; they are at a lounge in a somber mood. It finally sinks into their heads that they could be killed. All because of that trophy.

Sesay – "Last year's mess-up, and now this. We're risking our lives for what? A Trophy? Nobody even knows what happened to it! Ahggggg!"

P.M. Porto changes the subject to MARDI GRAS in New Orleans. No matter how tight you are, when it's Madi Gras time, it's time to party. TONIGHT, it's Madi Gras time. He finds the perfect Madi Gras Record.

(**Pak-o-way by the METERS**). Our cadets start hitting spoons on the table. Then P.M. Porto jumps up and starts dancing. Then another cadet starts dancing. More join in. In the end, everyone is dancing.

Two heavy women take over the dance floor. They are joined by two skinny guys. Their moves are uncanny.

Jan 11, 1991

Reveille. 05:00 Sergeant Quizzo appears - "Atten… hup. Pack your bags; you're leaving for **Saudi**. They pack with a nervous frenzy. A troop transport picks them up in front of their barracks. Sesay, " Now ya talking, a chauffeur." As they jump into the transport, they see the special para-gliders that they have used in training. The drive to the airport is short. They pull up to a Lockheed Martin C5-M Super Galaxy transport.

0.77.

The C-5 first entered service in 1970 in support of the Vietnam War; the Lockheed Martin C-5 Galaxy is the U.S. Air Force's only strategic airlifted. The largest aircraft in the branch's fleet, the C-5 Galaxy, can transport a 285,000-pound payload consisting of 6 Mine Resistant Ambush Protected vehicles (MRAPs) or 5 rotorcraft—a payload twice that of any other airlifter. Powered by four General Electric CF-80C2 turbofan engines, with each providing 50,580 pounds of thrust, the nearly 250 feet long C-5 Galaxy cruises at 500 mph. The 6955-mile trip to Saud Arabia should take approximately 15 hours.

Sesay is looking at the C5 - "Now I know how Pinocchio felt with "Monstro," the whale. You can get lost in here?. Monstro! That's your new name."

Departure from Fort Bragg

Jan 11, 1991   07:00 AM

Arrival at Elkan, Saudi

Jan 12, 1991   5:00 AM

They get flight orders from GOUND CONTROL, The C5 rumbles down the runway. Slow, then a little faster … the roar of the engines is getting louder, Monstro is getting faster … faster… faster **and takeoff**.

After the initial excitement subsides, the cadets settle down for the 15-hour, 6,955-mile flight to Elkan, Saudi Ariba.

Because of a favorable tailwind, It lands at Elkan, Saudi Ariba, on Saturday, Jan 12, 1991, at 4:15 AM

The Elkan Village Compound is a U.S. military compound located 20 kilometers south-east of Riyadh, Saudi Arabia

P.M. Porto is practicing his Kurdish. "**silav tu cawa diki**" How do you do?

"**Xwede, we re be**" God be with you." That's how I would talk to someone of authority. But if I'm greeting one of the locals, I would say "**tu li ku dere li babes.**" Sesay – "What does that mean?". P.M. – "**Where ya at, babes.**"

Sesay is listening. "It all sounds Greek to me." P.M. throws a tennis ball at him.

As they exit. "Monstro" and walk down the gang plank; they are overwhelmed by the activity at the base.

Sergeant Quizzo suddenly appears "Attennn Hut." The cadets are startled. How did he get on the plane and not be noticed for 15 hours? They rush and hug him. He pushes them away.

Jan 12,1991 04:20 AM Saudi Time

"Gentlemen, let's find our quarters and get some rest. Tomorrow is going to be hectic." After loading their equipment, they jump into the transport and munch on cold-cut sandwiches as they are driven to their tent. Within minutes they are all sleeping.

Jan 12,1991 05:00 AM Saudi time.

Reveille sounds, and Sesay jumps and hits his head on an overhead lantern. YUMA ARIZONA," he howlers. "A half an hour? … A HALF AN HOUR?". Aagggg."

Sergeant Quizzo appears. "Gentlemen, be ready for a mess at 05:30 AM."

After breakfast, Sergeant Quizzo takes them to a restricted area and shows the guard a special pass. They walk to a building that has even more security.

Jan 12,1991 10:00AM

Lieutenant Colonel Casey has just left a highly confidential meeting with Gen Schwarzkoph and enters the room.

Sergeant Quizzo "Attench Hut." Colonel Casey – "At ease. Please sit down. I have just left a briefing with the general. The air campaign will soon begin. But even before the initial air campaign starts, we will already deliver a serious blow to their defenses. "

"The Iraqi early warning system is Soviet-built Flat-Eye, Squat-Eye, and Spoon Rest intercept radar systems. They are arranged like a picket fence between Kuwait and Jordan. The two sights that we want to eliminate are due Northeast of a

Saudi town called **Arar**, some 300 miles northwest of King Khalid Military City, and just under the tri-border near **Wadi Al-Batin.**

The elimination of these sites will give us a 20-mile-wide corridor of unchecked air space into

Amar Iraq. Al-Batin

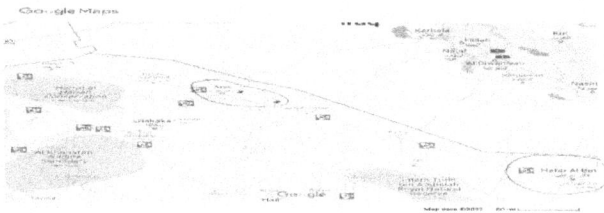

After reviewing Maximus plans, the following plan was submitted and accepted by General Schwarzkopf. Its name!

"OPERATION NORMANDY. "

Use Helicopters, Special forces, and GPS to eliminate the 2 Iraq Radar sites.

This new plan would be among the most tightly guarded secrets of the pre-war planning evolution. GPS was not widely known in Iraq, but it was operational,

STEALTH

The Air Force Special Operations Command's <u>MH-53J Pave Low III</u> Helicopters were best equipped for the job. Besides GPS, they also featured terrain-following radars, forward-looking infrared flying aids, and advanced threat detection and defensive systems. They themselves could make it to the radar sites without being detected, but they lacked the offensive punch needed to destroy them.

FIRE POWER

Now that a path-finding force was selected, a shooting force was actually needed to bring weapons to bear on the unsuspecting radar outposts. The obvious choice for this shooting force was the AH-64A Apache.

Accountability

The cadets would enter the Radar sites after the attack (unnoticed) and place the Chameleons on any targets that had not been destroyed by the Apache attack. The communications would be the first to be checked, followed by the Radar equipment, trucks, motorcycles, and other mobile equipment. Finally, the radar towers and any targets were not hit by the bombardment.

TIMING

The timing was everything; both radar sites had to be hit at the same moment. If one site went dark and the other site could get a call off to "command and control" in Baghdad, it could mean big trouble for fighter-bomber crews that would come later at (**H Hour-Jan 17,1991– 03:00)**

TEAM

The unhit targets had to be identified by GPS. This is where the **cadets** come into play. The Red Team(A) and the White Team(B) would sneak into the two Radar sites after the Apache attack and mark any unhit targets with chameleons.

The attack had to go exactly as planned; The Apaches would attack on (**Jan 17, 1991 – 02:35).** It should last not more than 4 minutes. **(02:35-02:39).** The Cadets would enter the camps at **02:40** and leave by **02:55.** They would then proceed to their pickup points.

At **02:59,** the Apache would unleash their fire power on the targets marked by the chameleons. At the same time, the Blackhawks would pick up the Cadets and return to Amar.

The full attack would fly through the two destroyed radar stations from **(Jan 17, 1991 – 03:00).** An initial strike force of F-15Es supported by EF-111 Ravens would pour in at a low level. They would be followed soon after by hundreds of other fighter attack aircraft.

Sergeant Quizzo brings out 60 Chameleons (10 for each cadet) and places them on a large table.

"Colonel Casey -" Cadets, a lot of people are putting their lives in your hands. You will be responsible for the mop-up of the two Iraqi radar stations close to the border. Your mission will be to jump from the Black Hawks 3 miles from the camps and use the Para-gliders to take you within a quarter-mile of the radar sites. There you will wait for the Apache attack and then enter silently into the two camps. At the camps, you will place the Chameleons on any targets that are not destroyed. Who is cadet Icon?" Maximus jumps up. "Sir!"

"Colonel Casey - "You will be responsible for the final setup of these devices." Colonel Casey hands Maximus an envelope. Sergeant! Takeover".

Sergeant Quizzo – "Attend hut." Colonel Casey leaves.

Sergeant Quizzo continues on with details of "Operation Normandy."

On this mission, the Chameleon will activate Red Tops.

Maximus opens the envelope while Sergeant Quizzo opens a box. It contains blue rods with a red glass top. It's definitely not a Blasting Caps.

Paul – "Why use Red-Tops and not blasting caps for detonations?"

Sergeant Quizzo – Blasting caps do not have enough explosive power. Also, "Weight! You have approximately 3-4 miles to carry yourself and the Chameleons. If you add the weight of the explosives, the para-gliders would be supporting way more weight than they were designed to carry. And second, the lighter load, the faster we can reach our objective.

As for these Red-Tops, they send out infer-red GPS signals, not frequency signals. Unless the enemy has infer-red detection equipment at these two sights, they won't know that anything is going on.

The Pave Low navigation equipment identifies this infer-red signal as a command and passes it, and its location coordinates to the accompanying Apache's Hellfire Missile or 50 caliber chain guns.

Maximus – "The Pave Low helicopters use the Forward-Looking Infrared system (FLIR) to tract and locate the infrared light from GPS Red-Tops. This light is invisible to the naked eye.

When the Hellfire Missile is activated, it travels at 995 mph or approximately 1459 fps. Assume your target is 3 miles away from the Apache. The time from the initiation of the command to the destruction of the target is about 10.8 seconds. The 50 caliber bullets travel at 3029 ft/sec or 2065 mph. They would cover the 3 miles in about 5.21 seconds. That's why it is so important to place the Chameleons in the right locations.

Here is some helpful information

Hell Fire   - time to 3-mile target 10.8 seconds

50 Caliber- time to 3-mile target 5.21 seconds

The plan is to fly the helicopters from Arar at the appointed time; Team A will fly towards Site 1 and Team B towards Site 2.

At the 3 miles from the targets, the Pave Lows will take final GPS readings of their site. The Black Hawks will ascend to 5000 feet and hover long enough for the cadets to jump and para-glide 3 miles to the targets. The Black Hawks will then land next to the Apache and wait for the "GO" signal.

The radar signature of the para-gliders will be zero, and their 40-50 mph air speed will be an exhilarating experience.

When teams reach their camp sites, they will wait for ¼ mile from the camp site until the first bombardment is finished. They will then enter the camp site and place Chameleons on the undamaged targets. They have less than 10 minutes to finish their job before the second bombardment will start. When they are finished, they will make it back 3 miles to the Black Hawks and take them back to the base.

Maximus reads the orders. "Each team will have 30 Chameleons.

1. Place the GPS Red-Top into the Chameleon's hole.

2.   Set all the Chameleons to TIME = 02:55. When a Chameleon is activated, the transmissions by their Red Top will be picked up by the Pave Lows receivers. Forty of the Chameleons will activate Hellfire missiles, while the other 20 will activate the Apache chain guns. One hundred rounds of 50 caliber bullets will shoot with one activation.

3. They very seldom miss.

4. Do not keep any activated Chameleons on your person. Remember you have

between 3-5 seconds from activation until impact. Play it safe and use 3 seconds.

"Quizzo – "We will place the Chameleons in the following order.

Communications	– 3 Hellfire each
Transport Trucks	- 1 Helphire each
Guns, Cannons	- 100 C50 each
Radar Towers	– 2 Hellfire's each

Ammo & Explosive s – 1000 C50 each

Sergeant Quizzo senses that the men are flat, with No energy. "Gentlemen, go rest until 18:00 tomorrow. Be ready for some practice."

On Jan 12, 1991, at 15:00, the meeting ended.

START OF PRACTICE

Jan 13,1991 18:00

At 18:00, the cadets are driven to a remote site on the camp. There are no overhead lights. No permanent living quarters, No permanent offices. All tents.

Sergeant Quizzo – "This compound is similar to stations 1 and 2. Notice the white squares. You will place chameleons set for Hellcat on the white squares marked Hellcat and place C50 Chameleons on white squares Marked C50. We don't want to waste a Hellcat on a machine gun

The Chameleons' you use tonight will have buzzers instead of Red Tops when they go off. Everyone takes six chameleons and puts them in a bag. When I say go, put the chameleon on the white squares. Go"

P.M. Porto is the first to reach a square. He has a C50 Chameleon in his hand. He forgets to set the time and activates it

three-second Later "BBZZZZZZZ." One hundred rounds from the C50 chain gun would have hit him. P.M. Higginbottom programs a Hellfire Chameleon to rotate 3 times before it can activate. He decides to change to a C50. In the process, he rotates the first chameleon 3 times. Five seconds later. "BBZZZZZZZ" He would be hit by a Hellfire missile. The next four minutes are a series of "BUZZZZZZ." Some are valid, and some are accidental. In all, 4 cadets would have been killed by their own actions. The cook tent was hit by 4 Hellcat missiles and 4300 rounds of 50C bullets.

Sergeant Quizzo – "I'm speechless."

Sesay – "Me too! No breakfast tomorrow!"

Someone throws a tennis ball at him.

Quizzo – Not for you; you were killed by a Hellfire. "We still have time. Tomorrow we will rise at 05:00 and begin again.

Jan14, 1991 05:00

Sergeant Quizzo "Gentlemen, After mess, we will practice all day and night if necessary.

From 06:00 to 12:00, they practiced full placements from 13:00 to 17:00 more practice. It is now June 14, 1991, at 18:00.

Sergeant Quizzo –"Gentlemen, The targets have been moved to different locations; You will have to be faster in order to place the Chameleons within the time limit. Let's get ready for some nighttime practice."

When they arrive at the camp, they see hundreds of chameleons and Red-Tops. They know they are in for a rough night.

Sergeant Quizzo "Gentlemen in front of you are what is called Night Vision Goggles. Put them on, but don't look directly at a light.

They are amazed. They can see, even in the dark."

Sesay – sings – "You light up life … "He's hit with a tennis ball. "Whoosss doing that???"

Sergeant Quizzo – "The rest of our practices will be done at night."

Jan 14,1991 19:00

They roam around the campsite, learning what they can do and what they cannot.

John Little walks into a tent with a lantern. He immediately jumps back out with a shout, "I've seen the Light." He's ignored.

Sergeant Quizzo assigns the first 60 chameleons.

"Gentlemen, tonight, the chameleons are loaded not with red tops but XK0 blasting caps. They are not exactly blasting caps but a firecracker. Any errors on your part may result in burnt fingers or worse. Keep your mask on,

"Ready Go"

Seven minutes later, it's over. All the Chameleons are placed and activated. Sergeant Quizzo's staff evaluates the results.

Three cadets singed (dead in actual combat), 3 radars destroyed, 1 communication transceiver destroyed, 3 transports destroyed, and 1 cook tent.

Jan 14,1991 19:30

Sergeant Quizzo assigns another 60 chameleons. "Ready Go"

Seven minutes later, it's over. Sergeant Quizzo's staff evaluate the results.

2 cadets singed (dead in actual combat), 2 Communication Transceivers destroyed, 4 Radar stations destroyed, 4 transports destroyed

Jan 14,1991 20:10

Sergeant Quizzo assigns another 60 chameleons. "Ready Go"

Six minutes later, it's over. Sergeant Quizzo's staff evaluate the results.

One cadet singed (dead in actual combat), and all Communication Transceivers, all Radar stations, and all transports were destroyed.

Sergeant Quizzo – "Gentleman, that's enough for tonight."

The men jump into the transport while Sergeant Quizzo and Paul Toscano speak on the side.

Sergeant Quizzo - "Paul, Higginbottom has killed himself in every practice exercise. In the real situation, he will deal not only with the chameleons but also with the enemy. I might have to remove him from the team."

Paul "We still have tomorrow."

Jan 15, 1991, 05:00

TO Al Jouf

On **January 15, 1991, at 5:00,** Colonel Casey's unit was ordered to deploy to Al Jouf. The attacking unit will fly from King Fahd Airbase to King Khalid Military City. After refueling, they will resume their flight northwest at a low altitude to a town called Amar. They arrived on January 15, 1991, at 13:00. This small airfield was approximately an hour's flying time to the starting point.

The total munitions for the 9 Apache Helicopters are:

72 Hellfire missiles,

171 Hydra 2.75-inch rockets

7200 to 9,000 rounds of 30-millimeter ammo

Colonel Casey will command two identical teams.

Each team will have

4 Apache gunships,

2 MH-53 Pave Lows,

and 21 Black Hawks.

3 Cadets (In the Black Hawks)

The extra Black Hawk is for backup.

On **January 15, 1991, at 13:00,** They arrived at Amar

TEAM A - Station 1 – Paul Toscano, Maximus Icon, P.M. Porto

TEAM B Station 2 - John Little, Sesay Swift, and Maximus Icon

Sergeant Quizzo – "Gentleman, let's go find our tent and unload our gear. Be prepared to move out at any time.

As the cadets unload their gear and sandstorm starts brewing. They barely manage to finish unloading when sergeant Quizzo informs them that the Mess is still open.

They fight through the blasts of sand and enter a tent that could hold 60 people. It's empty.

The private that's serving the food groans, "You guys must be important; we have T-bone steaks just for you. Sesay "How many?" Somebody hits him in the head with a tennis ball.

Each cadet is served a 16 oz T-Bone steak, Potato, Bread, Butter, and a dessert of their choice.

The talk at the table starts off with the mission and then changes to the Commander-In-Chief trophy.

Paul – "Guys, I would never have considered taking the Trophy if I thought it would have brought us to this. I love all of you guys, and I hope we all get back in one piece.

Sesay – "Hell with that! What happened to the Trophy?" John Little"- "Maybe Commander Dolin moved the Trophy before we got there?"

P.M. Porto – "Why would he do that with all that security equipment?"

As they get ready to leave the Mess, Colonel Casey steps into the Mess. "Gentlemen," They spring to attention. "At Ease. I want to express my gratitude for all the hard work you have put into this assignment. And I hope it will be successful.

Oh, by the way, an unsigned message just came across addressed to the "CADETS." It said, **"It is safe.** Do you know what that means?"

Chills run up John Little's spine. "Only somebody Big could send a message like that and have it delivered to a bunch of nobody's"

As they leave the Mess, the night storm makes for an eerie scene.

Jan 16   15:00

After MESS, the cadets start a "3 on 3" flag football game.

Team A – (Paul, Sesay, P.M.) vs. Team B – (John, Maximus, Chris).

Team A starts with the ball.

First play Paul tosses a bomb to P.M. – "TD."

It looks like a long day for Team B.

Team A Kicks off to Team B – Maximus runs the ball back to the 50-yard line. John is the quarterback. He calls a cross-play. The ball is snapped. The players cross, but John throws the ball up the middle into the waiting arms of Chris.

Startled, Chris takes off to the goal line at the speed of cold molasses. Sesay closes in on Chris, who panics and throws the ball up into the air. Maximus jumps and catches the ball and runs towards the goal. Paul and P.M. are laughing so hard that they can hardly run. Maximus scores.

Score -   Team A 6, Team B 6.

Jan 16   15:30

The PA system blares "Cadets Report to the meeting room."

Sergeant Quizzo – "Gentlemen = "Tonight we will do what we came he to do. Prepare your packs as if you were wounded and needed to stay alive for three days before help would arrive."

Sesay, "What if it takes more than 3 days?"
He's hit in the head with a tennis ball. He jumps and turns around. He sees nobody."

Sergeant Quizzo – "Gentlemen, the plan is very simple."

"Operation Normandy"

1 On **Jan 16, 20:00,** We fly from here to the starting point outside of Amar.

2 On **Jan 17 at 02:20,** The Black Halks rise to 4000 feet and release the cadets. Team A leaves for Site 1, and Team B leaves for Site 2.

They glide in and land ¼ mile from the sites and wait until after the first bombardment.'

3 At **2:35,** The first Apache bombardment begins. Four minutes of Hell. (It ends in 4 minutes)

4 At **2:40,** the Cadets enter stations A and B and set the Chameleons.

5 At **2:55,** The Cadets leave the stations and head back to the Black Hawks at the starting point.

6 At **2:59,** The Chameleons activate, and the second Apache bombardment begins.

7 At **03:00,** the air groups start flowing through the radar gap. At the same time, the Cadets head back to Amar.

Normandy Begins

Jan 17, 1991 - 0:30
The men are in their gear but laying around meditating on what tonight will bring.
Sergeant Quizzo enters the tent. "Gentlemen, Let's Go."
They jump up one of them gags and throw up. Nobody notices.

Team A (Paul, P.M., Sesay) head to their assigned helicopter.
Team B (John, Chris, Maximus) goes to the other helicopter.

89

One minute later, the teams are in the air. For 1 hour, the two teams travel from Amar to the starting point. It is now 1:30. The teams split and head toward their targets. At 2:15, the Black Hawks rise to 4000 feet and release the cadets. Like giant bats, they glide. The sound of wind filled with sand scrapes against the wings of the para-gliders. The sound is like concrete scraping against concrete.

At 2:20, the cadets land outside of the Iraqi camps. The next 10 minutes are tense. They can hear their hearts beat. And.... Pow Zap Zap Bang, it's 2:35. The first bombardment is in full swing. The cadets can see equipment being thrown around, buildings flying apart, flames rising from gasoline tanks, trucks being blown apart, and secondary explosions from ammunition. After 4 minutes, the bombardments stopped as fast as they started.
Paul, P.M., and Sesay move into Site 1

The smoke impairs their vision to approximately 50 feet. A swinging lantern is in front of each of the standing buildings. The storm intensity increases. One lantern falls from its hanging position and sets some boxes on fire. Immediately the door opens, and six IRAQ soldiers come out and start putting out the fire. P.M. Porto can see that this building is where the men eat and sleep. Also, he notices that these soldiers are not Republican Guards. These soldiers are conscripts.

P.M. speaks very loudly. **"ev rebere we yw netirse Sadum. Trvile poste bihele. He remale."**

They run to their trucks and leave.

Paul approaches P.M.. "What did you say to them?

P.M. - "This is your fearless leader, Saddam. Leave the post immediately. Go home. Leave everything."

Paul - "The other buildings must be the RADAR stations." While Paul and P.M. place the chameleons on the targets, Sesay notices something outside of the camp. He approaches the mound and lifts the corner of a large canvas. It's a SCUD missile. Twelve of them. Chris – "Paul, look what we have here! " Paul runs over to the Scuds.

Paul -" Place a chameleon here."

Sesay – "They have all been set."

Paul runs to one of the chameleons. Frustrated, he calls Sesay. "Where is a Hellfire Chameleon? Sesay points to two locations. Paul runs to the Chameleon closest to the Scuds. He places the Hellfire Chameleon on top of the scuds and removes the canvas. Time is running out.

Paul– "All of the chameleons should be set to activate at 02:59. Let's give everything one more check and get out of here.

At 02:50, they are finished and start the 3-mile walk to the wadi where they wait to be picked up by the Blackhawk.

Meanwhile, at 02:30 at Station 2

TEAM B John Little, Chris Higginbottom, and Maximus Icon. Station 2.

They are experiencing the fury of the night storm as they plow on. The sounds of the wind are eerie, and vision is distorted. It looks like rain, then bushes, then ghost-like figures, then like mounds moving back and forth. Three IRAQ soldiers are memorized. The mounds get closer and closer.

Our three cadets jump out of the storm. A fight ensues. No shots are fired, and after a fierce fight, our heroes win. They tie up and gag the three soldiers and proceed to the two buildings. The door of one of the remaining buildings is open.

They can see that this is the radar building. They place a Hellfire chameleon on the roof of the building. The other building must be the sleeping quarters. No one is in the radar building. They place a chameleon on top of that roof. The three soldiers they defeated must have occupied it. John and Maximus enter the radar building to dismantle the equipment while Chris proceeds to the other building. He constructs a door jamb so that the troops cannot get out. He then joins John and Maximus in the radar room.

They cut wires, pulled out chips, and set the timing to go off at 02:59. They leave the radar building and go around the camp, placing Chameleons at specific targets. All three look very tired. They notice a large mound covered with canvas.

Chris lifts the canvas "SCUDS."

"We have two chameleons left, and all of our targets are set.
Chris kisses the Chameleons and places them on the scud
pile.

John "Let's go." John, Chris, and Maximus head towards the
wadi

As they go over a dune, they see the lights of IRAQ troop
carriers coming at them. Hundreds of them. To make matters
worse, the storm is letting up, making it easier to see with the
FULL MOON. The first troop carrier has 4 men. Within
minutes, the IRAQ troops discover the tracks of the cadets.
They can easily determine the direction that the cadets take.
The chase is on.

John –"Chris, Maximus! Do you have your GPS with You?
"YES," The Iraq's are going to catch up with us soon if we
stay on the hard sand. We will scatter for 20 minutes and then
head towards the wadi. Use your GPS".

John and Maximus have chosen downhill paths on soft sand.
With each step, the sand shifts and covers their steps.

Unfortunately, Chris's path was on packed sand. His steps are
as clear as daylight.

The IRAQ Troops approach the spot where the cadets split.
Only Chris's tracks can be seen.

The IRAQ commander uses a searchlight on his tank to
search the ground. He is confused. Where did they disappear?
He notices something strange. The footprints head towards a
small depression in the sand and then stop. Six reeds are all in
a row and four feet apart. He silently signals to his
commander on the TANK.

With a positive nod, he commands his tank driver to roll over
the reeds.

The Storm increase as the TANK rolls over the first reed and then the second. When the tank rolls over the third reed, Chris screams. The commander starts to get out of the tank when his Radioman tells him that the SCUD missiles at Station 1 Must be moved from the site.

It is now 02:56

The commander jumps back into the tank and heads back to station 2.

Two minutes after the Iraq column leaves, the sand in the depression starts to move. Not where the tank tracks are, but 15 feet from the tracks, it's Chris.

He is now behind the column of tanks and trucks. He bumps into Maximus and John

John – "We were looking for you. Are you okay?" Chris – "Yes. Listen. They are going to remove the SCUDS from the site. Maximus "No Need. I already set the time on the chameleon. It will take care of itself.

It is now 2:58 and ticking.

John, Chris, and Maximus are a short distance from the wadi. The weather has turned clear.

Finally, they reach the wadi and are warmly greeted by Paul, P.M., and Sesay.

2:58:50

Their excitement grows as the second tick. 51, 52, ...59

2:59:00

The skyline was brightened by the explosions at Site 1 and Site 2.

They hear the gunfire from the Apaches. 40 Hellcats and 20 C50 chain guns are screaming over their heads.

Looking forward, they see explosion after explosion. Finally, one big burst that must have been the Scuds.

They are celebrating and don't see or hear the black hawk's motors.

The helicopter commander cannot get their attention. He also is caught up with the explosions.

After 3 minutes, the Blackhawk commander receives a call from Colonel Casey. "Why haven't you idiots taken off." "Sorry, Sir."

It's too late. The Apache and The Pave Lowe stay by the wadi.

The 20-mile path created by the cadets is open for business. The planes pour through. Over 812 sorties are flown that night.

At 06:00, Colonel Casey gets permission to fly back to the base. What a night!
As they are leaving, they hear the Tomahawk missiles flying overhead. They try to watch the fireworks, but fatigue sets in, and within minutes they are asleep.

Jan 17,1991 10:15

Our cadets arrive on the base at 10:15.

Sergeant Quizzo appears. "Gentlemen, Well done." They crush him with affection. After a 24-hour rest, "Monstro" returns them to the States.

Their involvement in Desert Storm is not common knowledge on the campus. They are not allowed to talk about it,

They are admitted back into the academy. Their time passes uneventfully until graduation.

General Yager has returned from Arabia and assumes his position as Commander of the academy.

Graduation Exercise

It's June 1, 1991. It's almost 6 months since the CID has gone missing. It's time for our hero's graduate.

The review begins. Army cadets are marching to the music of *John Phillip Sousa's* "Washington Post." Squad after squad of cadets march in precise cadence past the reviewing stand. The last squad, headed by Paul Toscano, halts before the reviewing stand and performs a close order drill.

A large American flag centers the squad as they march. The cadets halt in front of the reviewing stand and perform precise cadence. At each command, the flag is partially folded with a loud snap. Smaller and smaller the flag becomes. On the last command, the flag only covers a crate. The crate is lifted and, in all its glory, is

"THE COMMANDER IN CHIEF" trophy.

The reviewing stand goes wild. A thunderous roar is heard from the other cadets and ARMY brass, except for the Assistant Commandant De Witt.

Our heroes march on, but the CID remains in front of the reviewing stand.

From behind the CID and hidden from the Army staff, a thunderous cry "ARMY FIRST"! "ARMY FIRST. "

An officer in the reviewing stand stiffens and responds, "NAVY LAST."

THE END (Almost)

This event never happened, but it would have been fun if it did.

A Little Quiz to see if you were paying attention

1 Who were the cadets in 1955 that stole the Navy goat?

2 Who called Paul Toscano the night before the steal?

3 Who stole the CIC?

4 How was the CIC stolen?

5 How many baseballs were thrown at Sesay?

6 Where did our cadets get their Special training while in the U.S.?

7 What was Sesay's nickname for the plane that carried our cadets to Arabia?

8 Who was the 2nd string QB at Army that year?

9 Who sent the message "It is safe."

10 What was the score of the football game between our cadets.

Continue reading if you need help solving the Quiz

REPLAY OF

The Night of the Steal

Paul Toscano is on the phone at the FRONT-LINE lounge.
He hangs up the phone and leaves the lounge.

At a designated spot told by the anonymous phone caller,
Paul finds an envelope and opens it. "**Your plan is known.**"
Go to the phone booth on the corner and wait for a call."
When the caller asks, "WHO IS THIS," answer "1955". He
will tell you what to do.

Paul leaves the "FRONT LINE" and walks to the phone. It
rings. He answers. The caller says, "who is this"? Paul
answers "1955". The caller's reply's, "Meet me at the entrance
to the Naval academy in 3 hours and bring your old clothes.

Paul arrives at the entrance to the naval academy. A huge
sinister figure appears out of the dark. It's Frank (The
Superintendent). As they approach each other, Paul asks him
if he knows about the CIC. Not only did he know about
THE TROPHY, but he was mad that the NAVY always
seemed to have it in their possession.

When Paul confided that he had planned to steal the CIC,
they became friends. They then planned to use the City's
digging equipment and dig right under THE TROPHY and
take it. They proceeded to create a tunnel under the rotunda
and attach the necessary cables and packaging to move the
TROPHY. After 2 hours, the preparation was finished.
Cautiously the CID was brought to the surface and covered
at the end of the tunnel. The cadets will steal it tomorrow.
They shook hands and left. Thirty minutes later, Frank
returns and lifts the 270-pound trophy into the Crain bucket

and brings it to a waiting truck. The truck pulls off with the trophy, and Frank goes back and refills the tunnel under the rotunda.

Paul knows none of this.

On the night of the steal, Paul turns off the electricity, waits four minutes, and turns it back on. He walks into the rotunda and is captured by campus security.

GRADUATION EXERCISE REPLAY

It's June 1, 1991. It's almost 8 months since the CID has gone missing. It's time for our heroes to graduate. Frank Bluster arrives at West Point, pulling an electric cart with a large box. The cart is decorated to look like the Army Mule. He hands an envelope to the student officer and disappears. The cadet opens the letter and reads:

" Move the cart to the middle of Paul Toscano's squad. Open the flag and display it in the middle of the squad.

When the regiment stops in front of the reviewing stand, fold the flag and use it to lift the box.

The review begins. Army cadets are marching to the music of John Phillip Sousa's "Washington Post." Squad after squad of cadets march in precise cadence past the reviewing stand. The last squad, headed by Paul Toscano, halts before the reviewing and performs a close order drill.

A large American flag centers the squad as they march. The cadets halt in front of the reviewing stand and perform precise cadence. At each command, the flag is partially folded with a loud snap.

Smaller and smaller the flag becomes. On the last command, the flag only covers the crate. The crate is lifted and in all of its glory is:

"THE COMMANDER IN CHIEF" Trophy.

An unseen voice vibrates from the crowd - "Army First," "Army First," Army First," " Army First," Gen Yager stiffens and responds, "Navy Last," "Navy Last," Navy Last," " Navy Last."

The two eyes meet.

Phineas and Yag.
They've done it
again.

END 2

CURRENT STATUS OF OUR HEROES

John Little –
    Promoted to Capitan and heads Virginia Military
    Institute.

Maximus Icon – Maximus works for a major Corporation. He
    owns most of the patents for a product called "The
    electric bunny car."

P.M. Porto – Interpreter at the United Nations.

Sesay Swift - Writer for TV Comedy show

Chris Higginbottom - Works at a fireworks manufacturing
    plant.

Frank T Bluster (Phineas) – Still working for the city and
    griping about the NAVY.

Capitan Charles Simms De Witt – Reassigned to Virginia
Military Institute. Works under Captain John Little.

Paul Toscano – Current teacher at Seal Team 6

General, E.G., Yager – Retired and raises goats and mirlitons.

THE END 3

Research Article

JALOPNIK – The Real Hero's

Desert Storm's Opening Shots Came From This Daring Helicopter Raid 25 Years Ago Today

By
Tyler Rogoway
1/17/16 5:20 PM
Comments (135)

You have to kick down an enemy's front door somehow, and in the case of Operation Desert Storm, novel use of AH-64A Apache and MH-53J Special Operations Pave Low helicopters did just that for their fast-flying fighter jet comrades. The top-secret mission was dubbed Task Force Normandy, and it occurred 25 years ago today.

Operation Desert Storm By The Numbers On Its 25th Anniversary

Twenty-five years ago today, President George H.W. Bush announced the execution of Operation Desert

Read more

The thought that a critical portion of Iraq's elaborate radar "fence" was blinded by helicopters seems strange in this day and age of stealthy standoff weaponry. But 25 years ago today, the choices for kicking open a hole in Iraq's radar defenses weren't so plentiful. The fact that these sites were located in the vast, featureless desert along the border of Saudi Arabia and Iraq made the task even more challenging.

Related Stories

This 2000 Acura Integra Type R On Bring A Trailer Is Another Dark Sign Of The Times
Harley-Davidson Is Bringing King Of The Baggers Excitement To The Road
Rivian Looking For A Production Rebound After Miserable 2021

Originally, it was briefed to General Schwarzkopf, the larger-than-life four-star General that would head the war, that special forces would be deployed to the radar sites and take them out the old-fashioned way by raiding them. Another plan had these operators laser-designate the sites for attack aircraft to strike. The General rejected these plans due to the inherent risk of ground forces being compromised by unforeseen factors.

Cruise missiles could have done the job, but nobody would have had eyes on the targets to make sure they were totally destroyed. It would have been disastrous if one of the sites were thought to have been destroyed, just for it to go back online while the skies were full of approaching coalition aircraft.

Instead, less traditional tactics would be required, ones where the strike force could make sure the radar sites were left in rubble. This new plan would be among the most tightly guarded secrets of the pre-war planning evolution.

At the time, there were few Global Positioning System units available in the field, and far fewer integrated into an aircraft's navigational suite. The pinpoint navigation needed to find two Iraqi radar stations, located about 70 miles apart, without having the benefit of major landmarks or daylight, and all by surprise, left war planners to tap an unlikely team of helicopter crews to get the job done.

By the time planning was underway for Desert Storm, the Air Force Special Operations Command's tricked-out MH-53J Pave Low III Helicopters had been outfitted with the most capable navigational suite on any aircraft in the world. It included GPS that would be as accurate over thousands of square miles of shifting sands as they were over a major city. They also featured terrain-following radars, forward-looking infrared flying aids, and advanced threat detection and defensive systems. They themselves could make it to the radar sites without being detected, but they lacked the offensive punch needed to destroy them.

Now that a path-finding force was selected, a shooting force was actually needed to bring weapons to bear on the unsuspecting radar outposts. The obvious choice for this shooting force? The most advanced attack helicopter in U.S. service that was adapted specifically to fly and fight at night was the AH-64A Apache.

In the early fall of 1990, training began for this unique mission. Over the next few months, no less than six live-fire drills were practiced to evaluate the Apache's ability to take out the targets and the Pave Low's ability to get them there. The timing was everything; both sites had to be hit at the same moment. If one went dark and the other could get a call off to command and control in Baghdad, it could mean big trouble for fighter-bomber crews.

All the training occurred while deployed to Saudi Arabia for Desert Shield, the precursor to Desert Storm. The Air Force-Army team made up of the 20th Special Operations Squadron and the 1st Battalion, 101st Aviation Regiment of the 101st Airborne worked out all the details, including speeds, altitudes, communication (which there really was none aside from glow-sticks dropped out of the MH-53s for position updates), and especially contingencies.

The plan was that each site would be struck by one of two teams, the Red Team and the White Team. These teams would consist of one MH-53J that would use its high-end navigational suite and terrain-following radar to pave the way for each team of four Apaches.

These Apache would be loaded with eight AGM-114 Hellfire missiles, 19 70mm hydra rocket pods, a full load of 30mm ammunition, and a 1,700-pound, 270-gallon external fuel tank. The tanks had never been used before and were an innovation from the mission. Although they put the Apaches over gross combat weight, they would make it so they would not have to refuel in Iraq via a temporary forward refueling base. A stigma over such a tactic still remained since it was used with fatal consequences during Operation Eagle Claw, the doomed mission to rescue American hostages held in Iran over a decade earlier.

Additionally, a UH-60 Black Hawk would also be available for contingency search and rescue operations, and one spare Apache would be available if one of the prime forces of eight

Apaches had a problem before the infiltration into Iraqi airspace began.

About just a couple dozen miles from reaching their targets, the MH-53s would break off and head to a future rendezvous point, while the Apaches would update their navigation system one more time and make their final push to the radar sites.

The plan had to go exactly as briefed, with missiles landing on the radar sites 22 minutes before H-hour, which was scheduled for 3 AM. In doing so, a 20 or so mile-wide corridor would be blown open in Iraq's overlapping early warning radar network, and an initial strike force of F-15Es supported by EF-111 Ravens would pour in at a low level. They would be followed soon after by throngs of other fighter attack aircraft.

All involved would be tested to the max, flying a round-about route to their targets following the contour of the earth for long periods of time, much of which would be devoid of anything but sand. Even with night vision infrared optics, this would be no easy feat. Flying at 120 mph, about fifty feet of altitude, would be the operational norm for the mission, and since they had never flown over the terrain in question before, it would be all new to them.

Just a couple of days before the mission occurred, the force was forward deployed to Al Jouf Air Base, a small airfield in western Saudi Arabia. Even this had to be done in a stealthy manner so as not to alert Iraqi intelligence. From there, they would launch their assault in the coming days, should they be called to do so.

The assault was ordered for the night of the 17th of January, and the Pave Lows, with Apaches in tow, crossed over into Iraq airspace at 2:12 AM, just 48 minutes before H-hour was scheduled. Both teams made their way toward their targets, during which nothing out of the ordinary occurred. In fact, it was so calm that it was almost alarming to the crews. Both Pave Low teams hit their last way-point upon which the Apaches broke off to start the war.

Both teams of AH-64 Apaches approached their radar station targets, and just outside of three miles, they went into a hover and fine-tuned their targeting. The only communications sent during the entire infiltration were transmissions from the Apache forces shortly after simultaneously firing their first missiles. "Party in ten" was broadcast by the lead Apache pilots; the code for reporting the first impacts from their Hellfire was ten seconds from occurring.

Ten seconds later, power generator vans appeared as blooming white splotches on the Apache crews' FLIR screens. What followed next was a barrage of weaponry and ammunition that obliterated the radar stations wholesale. The Apaches swooped ever closer as they kept firing their weapons. Anti-aircraft guns went up like fireworks, radar dishes were shattered into tiny pieces, and Iraqis could run for their lives. In total, 27 Hellfires, 100 rockets, and 4000 rounds of 30mm ammunition were fired at the sensor outposts from what must have seemed like fire-breathing black holes in the night sky by the unfortunate souls on the receiving end of the attack.

The war had begun, and just minutes later, nearly 100 coalition fighters would barrel through the blind hole in

Saddam's radar defenses and onto their targets deep in Iraq. General Schwarzkopf later remarked that the Apaches "plucked out the eyes" of Iraq's border defenses.

On their way back toward the Saudi border, as both teams of Apaches rejoined with their Pave Low teammates, they radioed simply "Nebraska AAA" and "California AAA." This meant that the generators were knocked out, the sites were obliterated, and there were no friendly losses. It was a clean sweep.

Still, the mission was not over; as they made their way back towards the border, low-flying fighters screamed overhead in the opposite direction. There were some fears that a mistake could be made and that these jets could see the comparatively slow-flying helicopter force heading in their opposite direction as an enemy one.

This did not occur, thankfully, but Iraqi ground units were now aware that something big was happening. SA-7 shoulder-fired heat-seeking missiles were fired on the Pave Lows, although their defensive countermeasures and hard maneuvering worked to evade being struck by them. In the end, everyone returned unscathed.

The historic and highly successful Task Force Normandy remains one of the best examples of applying unique military capabilities to a challenging target set in a creative way. Not only that, but the fact that the first shots of Desert Storm were fired by helicopters is a testament to rotary-wing air power and just how flexible it can be with the right vision.

Contact the author at Tyler@jalopnik.com.

Movie Ending

THE NEXT END (Movie Ending) version.

Play the John Phillip Susa SONG "Washington Post" and show Cadets Marching from World War 1 to the present times as the credits are running. Show the current picture of the general and how he looked in 1955. (10 seconds)

As the credits appear, they are displayed on the right side of the screen,

Music Plays – "Get down tonight" by KC and the sunshine band

On the left side of the screen, each actor shows his dance steps. (10 seconds each)

This includes not only our main characters but anyone on the movie set that wants to dance.

Actors, Iraq Soldiers, Camera Men, Everybody on the set.

Groups of cast members, and anything else that can be thought of.

The object is to get the movie audience to be dancing as they leave the theater.

END 4

My Comments:

All during the movie, good R & B songs are played.

No Cursing or obscenities or religious references. Violence is shown in a comical way. Do not actually show any IRAQIS being killed. They will be either knocked out or flee.
The movie must obtain a PG or PG13 Rating.
  The tone of the movie should be like an Errol Flynn movie. (Robin Hood) or an Indiana Jones movie. (You know that the cadets are going to win).

Action should limit the number of explosions but emphasize individual or group action. There will be a need for dance choreography.
A ballroom brawl (John Wayne - Port of the Seven Sinners)
The assistant commander (Captain De Witt) must be someone that you love to hate. He cannot be too comical. "DABNEY COLEMAN"

The leader of the sophomore cadets (Reginald Wadsworth) must be a snob but not a fool.

THE END

Think of current actors to play these movie parts.

John Little –
Maximus Icon –
P.M. Porto –
Sesay Swift -
Chris Higginbottom -
Frank T Bluster (Phineas) –
Capitan Charles Simms De Witt –

Paul Toscano –

General, E.G., Yager (Yag) –

Commander Dolan -

Captain Casey -

Sergeant Quizzo -

Seared Tivoli -

Reginald Wadsworth –

Call Hollywood.
Tell them to make me an offer I can't refuse.
Make me wealthy before I die.

www.ingramcontent.com/pod-product-compliance
Lightning Source LLC
Chambersburg PA
CBHW071745200326
41519CB00021BC/6870